Creatures of the Current is an environmental fantasy.

Written in narrative prose, and seamlessly interspersed with lyrics, it lends itself to the performance genre of a twenty-first century Earth Folk Ballad, fusing far-flung sounds and movements across dimensions.

The story, which is in seven brief episodes, has been used on several occasions at various locations, and using various media, to conduct theatre readings, workshops and awareness on biodiversity and sustainable development, and to enhance a global biodiversity planning process.

Creatures of the Current has been discussed by an informal Book Club in Delhi's National Capital Region.

A training company has interviewed the author over a series of internet meetings, for insights into the text, and on how to incorporate its use in theatre and training.

Creatures of the Current was on the writer's poetry blog, Junglessence, using the pen-name of Quill-o-the-Wisp (with the identity of the poet also mentioned on the blog), for approximately five-and-a-half years, beginning in November 2008.

It was published as an eBook on Kindle in July 2014, followed by the paperback version on Create Space in 2015.

The key to the planet's future, that the reader now handles!

THE JOURNEY BEGINS

      WE MEET THE FOREST PEOPLE

    THE GHARIAL AND THE WATER CREATURES

LICKETY-SPLIT!

      WE MEET THE THICKET AND GANG

THE CITY OF HAZAARBAZAAR

        THERE'LL BE A RADICAL CHANGE

THE JOURNEY BEGINS

Far away from all of us, the Bahtareen river winds its whimsical way. Coloured blue, or green, or pink by the passing light, it makes its rendezvous with jutting rocks.

Cutting edges, and throwing up waves of bubbles, it alternates between a murmur and a roar, a solitary plink and a repertoire of plonks.

The river Bahtareen creates many banks. The Banks of the World are, indeed, carved by its rivers. On the upper banks of the Bahtareen, deep in the Hurryburry jungle, lives Antaratma, the river-guide.

Jai, Raj, Diya and The Lady Who Does Not Like Air Conditioners were in search of someone who would guide them along the river. Few people had ever met Antaratma, the river-guide. But his ability to guide people through their journeys was talked about in many lands.

The group set out to look for Antar. As it grew dark, people became shadowy forms. The shadowy forms steered them to the edge of the jungle of Hurryburry.

Through the mazes of the jungle of Hurryburry they stumbled, finding themselves drawn to the abode of Antar. He met them outside his hut. They could hear the gurgle of the Bahtareen from his dwelling.

"We'd like to journey along this river on your raft," they said. "There are river-rapids," he answered, and taught them how the rapids must be run. He was strong and had a deep voice that shook the raft.

"Is everyone ready, then?" he asked.
"Yes!" they all replied.
"Now, let's see if you can remember what I told you!" prompted Antar.
They all sang with him,
"This is the hull
And this is the stern,
-the front and the back of the raft.
Paddling along the river is fun,
But there's something to learn of the craft."

Jai, Raj, Diya and the lady were in a hurry to clamber on to the raft.

"Oh! Before I forget," said Antar, "The entire raft could capsize...topple over, you know."

"Oh, I see," said the lady.

"But the river runs through a forest," he continued, "It's the greenest, the darkest, the densest, the star-kissed...."

The river, with its promise of unknown destinations, was tempting. The lady decided that they should carry on with the journey.

"Let's go, everyone!" she called, much to the relief of Jai, Raj and Diya, who were beginning to get a little impatient.

"How clean the air is on this faraway river," said Raj, as the calm Bahtareen flowed beneath their raft. They breathed in and out and out and in. The mixed scents of the river, the passing rocks and the land-bound forest flowed into them and surrounded them. Reflections from the water bounced on to their skin and eyes. The sun's rays fell on them, refracted through globules. Droplets of the crystalline Bahtareen splashed through their hair.

"Where does this river go to?" wondered Jai.

"It flows through these beautiful jungles and places that nobody has ever seen," said the lady. "And then it flows past cities and towns till it finally reaches the ocean."

They crossed a few children who waved at them from the banks of the river. "Ta ta, ta ta!" the children from the forest called.

"Ta ta!"

Jai, Raj and Diya waved back.

"Those kids live in the forest," said Antar, "I hear there's a lot of magic in these woods."

"When are we going into the woods?" Diya wanted to know.
"We're already there," laughed Antar.
"Where's the magic?" Diya asked him.
"It's all around," explained the lady, "It takes one a while to recognize it."

"Where has this river come from?" asked Jai.
"From icy mountaintops," said the lady.

With a little warmth, the snow melts on lofty mountains, forming numerous joyous springs. Into the slipstream of these springs, are drawn minerals and herbs whose juices lend the hope of immortality to the rivers that flow thenceforth.

A breeze had woken the shore-bound birds from their slumber and had unfurled the wild flowers to broadcast the seeds and the pollen of the jungle of Hurryburry.

It was the Halchalhawa. An urgent breeze with a purpose. It struck the faces of Jai, Raj, Diya and the grown-ups. The Halchalhawa was known to wrench ribbons that bound tresses, entangling dense locks in a mass of freedom.

The Halchalhawa rocked the raft while the river guide shouted instructions for them to keep it from toppling.

"Ha! Ha! This is like a rocking horse!" laughed Diya who was enjoying the ride, unmindful of its hazards.

"We're nearing the first rapid!" shouted Antaratma, the river-guide. "Those on the right, paddle backwards, we need to take a left turn!" "A left turn!" they all shouted. "All forward now!" yelled Antar. "All forward!" they all screamed, "Wow!" this is fun!" "Brace yourselves!" yelled Antar, "This is a difficult patch!" Then, there were mixed sounds of "Help!- my paddle- oh no!- I'm falling- river-guide, where are you!- he's fallen off too- point your toes down-river! point your toes down-river!"

They were all thrown off the raft and onto the waves. Antar had told them to relax and let the river carry them if the raft capsized.

By evening, the Bahtareen had carried them all to a shady spot on its banks. They were deep inside the jungle of Hurryburry.

WE MEET THE FOREST PEOPLE

A greenish darkness seeped into the Bahtareen. It mingled with the foliage of the Hurryburry. The Shadows of Sham thus slunk into the jungle, there to encounter the Halchalhawa. Halchal, in a relaxed moment, stretched lazily from bough to bough, stirring a few wakeful leaves.

Gusty Halchal caused the Shadows of Sham to shiver momentarily. Then Jai, Raj and Diya heard the distant hum of human voices. The hum seemed to be a song, sung in indistinguishable, strange tongues. The lady and the river-guide were anxious to seek out civilization.

They walked cautiously towards the music. It wafted from the vicinity of a cluster of mud huts with thatched roofs that were embedded in the earth.

About a hundred human beings were dancing to a rhythmic beat. Old and young, fat and thin, men and women, tall and short, they were all there. They formed circles and patterns and rows as they danced and clapped and sang. They wore only leaves and flowers and shells.

It was dark except for a strange lamp that stood near a thatched cowshed. There were cows and buffaloes and bulls who were all asleep.

"Who are these people?" Raj asked Antar in a whisper. "Do they live in those huts?" Jai wanted to know.

"They are forest people," Antar informed them in a whisper, "Yes, they live in those huts."

"Look at those bows and arrows," exclaimed Diya in an excited voice.

"Will they attack us?" asked Jai, sounding worried.

"I hope not," answered Antar. "Of course not," said the lady, "They are simple, nice people." They might feel scared of us." "You can never tell...." said Antar, and Jai gathered the impression that Antar was only joking, which was, indeed, partly correct.

Suddenly, a dog barked, and the revelry in the village came to an abrupt halt.

"What is it?" the forest-people asked each other. There were mixed sounds of "There's someone here- where?- that way!" They all looked towards the bush that hid the group.

Antar the river-guide pushed his way forward, asking the others to follow.

"Hello!" he called, "It's us. We're from the world outside."

"Step into our world, strange ones!" said the people whose village it was.

"It's dark, and there's no electricity," complained Raj.

"Where are the lights?" asked Diya, looking doubtfully at the gobar-gas lantern.

"How do you survive without electricity?" Jai asked the hundred people who had been dancing and who were now listening to him.

"How do you survive without electricity?" he asked again, thinking they might not have understood his question. But they had. They twisted themselves into celestial shapes as they chanted in unison,

"The stars and the moon and the sun are all bright.
They light up the morning, the evening, the noon and the night.
O Sun.
Burning like fire.
It's fire, it's fire, it's fire...
Aspirations. Aspirations.
The fire is bright.
The fire is light.
It lights up the morning, the evening, the noon and the night.
Burning like fire, like fire, like fire."

The oldest from amongst them, a lady with flowing black hair, was deep in concentration. Fluorescent light glowed from her, strobe-like, till the dance was concluded.

"It looks like you're quite happy without our electric stars," said Antar. A sheepish tone had stolen into his remark.

"Well, I guess one could do without power," conjectured the Lady Who Did Not Like Air Conditioners.

"Might be fun, come to think of it," mused Antar, "Might be fun, come to dream of it...."

"No electricity?" asked Jai incredulously.

"No electricity!" repeated the village of a hundred people.

"None," yawned a sleepy cow from the shed.

"No electricity!" they sang.
"At least not the kind you have in mind.
Solar power is what we use.
We've got our own science and our own special views...."

"Your own special views?" asked Diya. She was still looking at the forest lady who had been fluorescent a few moments ago.

"Yes. We keep the river clean and respect the waves that lap along its banks," said the fluorescent lady in a bright voice.

"We keep the river clean!" the village chanted, and offered them pots of water to drink. Then, they began a slow dance that flowed with the soft melody that they summoned. To this, they added words,

"The rain and the river, the storm and the dew,
They quench us and soothe us and make us feel new.
O H2O.
Streaming clear water.
Clear water, clear water, clear water.
It's getting hotter.
Where is the water.
Hotter and hotter.
The water is blue.
The water is you.
It's three-fourths of the earth and four-fifths of you.
Flowing like water.
Like water, like water, like water."

The gurgle of the Bahtareen was audible as splinters of golden moonlight crossed its crests.

"Please tell us about the air we're breathing," Jai requested, inspired by the proximity of the elements, "It feels different here."

The Halchalhawa rustled through their leafy garments and garlands of flowers. The Shadows of Sham shuddered in the jungle of Hurryburry. The forest people began uttering words into the atmosphere, creating ripples that still move and travel, and catch us, perhaps, as we tread through our lives.

They chanted,

"The wind and the gale, the breeze and the air,
They cross over boundaries and reach everywhere.
O Air.
Breezes that blow.
O, o-o,. O, o-o, O, o-o...
Oxygen flow, with the breezes that blow.
Oxygen. Oxygen.
There are fumes in the air that weren't always there.
Through our homes and our lungs, they creep everywhere.
Breezes that blow.
O, o-o, O, o-o, O, o-o..."

Antar noticed that little Diya's perspective had tuned into these ideas with ease. But there were perplexed looks on the faces of Jai, Raj and the lady. He understood the confusion of the city dwellers.

"The earth. Let me tell you about the earth," he said on a sudden impulse.

Everyone turned towards him. The deep chords of his voice jolted them from their dream-like state, measuring seven point eight on the richter scale.

That was a moment that heralded the crumbling of the gluttonous bastions of urban creation. Antar's voice vibrated as he sang,

"There are rivers that wind from the mountains to the plains.
There are places where snow falls, and at places, it rains.
There are places like this one, with jungles and streams,
With people who think and dance like our dreams.
And there are places all jammed with factories and cars,
With so much of smoke that you can't find the stars.
But there are people there too,
Like me and like you
Who love the wind and stars
But need the trains and cars.
Who splash through puddles when it rains,
And muddle through muddles in their brains."

"What do we do?" asked Raj.

Jai, Raj, Diya and the lady walked about, muttering, "What do we do? What do we do?" in a dazed fashion. They kept bumping into each other and tripping on gnarled roots. This was no dance.

"Keep journeying down this magical river and you might find an answer," said the village of a hundred people through a telepathic message that intruded their trance-like state.

Antar, who had been watching this last scene, was pleased. "Thank you!" he said.

"Thank you!" repeated the children and the lady.
"May the spirit of the jungle protect you!" said the village.
"And you!" called the group.

They found their raft, and were back on the river.

THE GHARIAL AND THE WATER CREATURES

Here, the river was calm and wide and deep. They paddled their way through the moonlit water. On the banks of the Bahtareen, giant hills rose into the Shadows of Sham. Silhouetted by the full moon, the hills of the Hurryburry watched them as they paddled.

The night looked beautiful, but the hills of the Hurryburry did not look happy. The Halchalhawa sighed a sad sigh, sending a chill through everyone's spines.

Suddenly, the children, who were the only people on the raft who were awake, heard a loud splash. It was louder than a splash. It wasn't exactly a splash-splash. It sounded like the gurgle of an elephant stepping out of a cauldron of hot chocolate.

From under the water, appeared a gigantic green creature. It had eyes that gleamed in the moonlight, sharp rows of teeth and scaly skin. Only half of its long, horizontal body was visible above the water.

"Don't be afraid, I'm just a friendly crocodile."

Inspite of the darkening alleys of the Bahtareen, he maintained that he was a friendly crocodile, a gharial in those parts.

"And I don't eat human beings yet," he assured them, with an amused grin.

"Not yet?" asked Diya, wondering why that didn't sound as reassuring as it was meant to.

"We only eat people when all the other food disappears," explained the gharial.

"What's all the other food?" asked Jai skeptically. He had heard stories of crafty crocodiles.

"Umm," said the gharial, "I like those little fish, and some algae. Other juicy stuff from the river."

"Where do you live?" asked Diya. She saw he wasn't carrying his house keys.

"In the river," said the gharial, "I like lounging along the river banks on sunny afternoons."

"And are all the water creatures frightened of you?"

"Not always," replied the gharial. "I only look for food when I'm hungry."

"Poor little fish," said Diya in a stern voice.

"Oh, they don't mind, really. You know, they aren't around to worry about me once I've eaten them up!" laughed the gharial.

"Ooo, I'm scared of you," said Diya, moving closer to Jai and Raj.

"Don't be afraid," said the gharial, "Come, let me take you children to our Monthly Water Creatures' Full Moon Association meeting."

Raj and Diya looked at Jai. They wanted to go on a gharial ride, but it depended on Jai who was the eldest.

"Er- ahem," the gharial cleared his scaly throat, "I'm the president of the association," he revealed, hoping that would impress Jai.

Jai was wondering whether he should wake up the lady and Antar to ask for permission. But he was too polite to wake up people who were fast asleep.

The gharial made the decision for them, "Oh, don't wake up the lady and the river-guide. We're a little suspicious of grown-up humans," he confided.

"Come, hop onto my back," urged the gharial.

Jai was curious about the water creatures' meeting. He felt sure that they were going to be the first human beings to ever attend such a meeting.

"Ah, there, you've already learnt the knack," said the gharial, pleased to see that Jai had decided to go on the little adventure with his little friends.

"And we're off to follow the river to a cave.
Oh, I'll bring you back before they rant and rave.
Oh, don't you worry 'coz we'll be back,
And I won't convert any of you into my little snack."

The gharial, who usually moved slowly was a trifle excited. His glittering eyes rolled back to catch a glimpse of the children.

"When does all your other food disappear so that you have to eat humans?" Diya asked.

"When the river is dirtied by human beings, and when they tamper with the river, all the creatures in it suffer. Sometimes they die. See, a big guy like me could starve for days if all the fish and ummmm tasty little snails start dying."

"You're weird," said Diya.

"Not really," replied the gharial, "My teeth and my intestines are meant for eating such stuff. Give me a break. That's how I've been created...all of us destroy creatures and things for our own food and shelter...human beings are the most destructive, though. You know what I mean?"

"You mean like cutting trees to build houses?" asked Jai.

"Yes, something like that," replied the gharial, "But the important thing is to not be greedy. We must help ourselves only to what we need, and no more."

The gharial swam swiftly through the water. He could tell by the shadows thrown by the full moon, that he would be late for the meeting. A cave full of creatures would be waiting for him.

"Mr. Gharial, this is my first gharial ride," said Diya.

"And not your last one, hopefully!" joked Jai in a half-whisper.

"Al, can we call you Al?" he asked loudly, so that the gharial could hear him.

"You can call me Al," laughed the gharial, who was not an alligator, but a crocodile.

"What's so funny?" asked Diya.

"Never mind!" said the gharial. Then he changed his mind, and said, "You can call me Agarmagar, that's my name. Thank you very much."

"So Agarmagar, you're a gharial which is a kind of crocodile," concluded Jai.

"Ha ha, wasn't that clever!" chortled Agarmagar.

They could hear the mixed buzz of countless water-creatures in the hidden darkness.

The Shadows of Sham were heavy here. Agarmagar was thinking about the water-creatures. He hadn't done his homework for the meeting, as usual. But he was concerned.

"Well, Agarmagar, what's this water creatures' meeting all about?" asked Jai.

"You'll see. It's a big secret I'm letting you all into. The creatures are worried," Agarmagar whispered through watery bubbles. Then, a sudden thought struck the scaly Agarmagar. "Maybe we could use your help," he announced.

Ahead of them, one string of the river pulled away from the mainstream and entered a cave. This was the route that Agarmagar now followed.

"Sorry, this is a narrow branch of the river," he apologised, "It squeezes through bushes and reeds to find the cave. Here we are!"

The buzz, hiss, quack and croak of the countless water creatures had been growing louder as he spoke. Now, they entered the watery cave. A charged silence filled the cave that had been echoing with the heated voices of the water creatures.

The countless water creatures watched as Agarmagar, the president of their association, swam in with the three children perched on his back.

News travels fast on the Bahtareen, and it had whizzed through the Shadows of Sham, a-sail on the Halchalhawa, into the Cave of Creation.

Moonlight reflected off the water, illuminating all that was substantial. The walls, the inner dome and the shallow parts of the cave were packed with water creatures.

Electric eels, water snakes, frogs, schools of fish, ducks, even dolphins and otters had found their way to the meeting. Those who could, clung to the walls for an inch of space, helped by the suction of their limbs and digits. There were snails and crabs, prawns and turtles. They plastered even the jagged edges of the cave.

"We welcome you to the fifty-fourth meeeting of our asssociation.
We are the prrroud but trrroubled creeeatures of the rrriver!!"
they hollered, in a cacophony of voices.

"Many moons have gone by
But things get worse although we trrry...."
croaked a puffed-up frog who wanted to sound important.

Jai couldn't help noticing that the frog sounded just a little bored. But he seemed to want to please Agarmagar. He carried a bunch of files for Agarmagar to peruse.

"We've got newsss from ssssleuthsss down-river.
Neeews that should certainly make you shiver...."

hissed a watchful water-snake. She didn't seem to be too terrorized by Agarmagar like many of the others were. But she knew that he was mightier than most of them.

"There are so many chemicals making the water black.
I drank it yesterday, and felt a little slack. Slack. slack."
quacked the main duck, practically hysterical.

Agarmagar was quick to catch the point.

"Who spews these poisonous chemicals into our water?" he bellowed.

"It's the waste from those factories," screamed each frog, prawn, fish, otter, duck, dolphin, turtle, snake and flamingo that was there.

"Dangerous stuff?" inquired a quickly infuriated Agarmagar.

"Dangerous stuff!" replied the countless creatures in the Cave of Creation.

"But guesss what we've found out. They've invented a machine that cleans tonnes of water. Makes it reeeally cleeean."

"There you are, then. Isn't that the solution? Ha ha! Wasn't that clever," responded Agarmagar who hadn't done his homework.

"Sssolution indeeed! They're ssso, ssso ssselfffish,
And insssissstent is their greeed," hissed the water snake.

"They're too unconcerned to take the trrrouble,
They say their costs will only double," explained the frog.

Agarmagar was deftly absorbing the information. The Cave waited for the plan of action.

Finally, the hysterically practical duck said,
"Tell us all, have we run into some luck?
Will our little guests help us to clean up the muck?"

Agarmagar knew that the time had come, to take some action. Any action. And here was a novel idea.

He rolled his glittering eyes back to look at Jai, Raj and Diya, addressing them so that the countless creatures could hear his speech,

"Children, by now, you know what the matter is.
We're not just creatures from a wildlife quiz.
We're real, and we belong to the water.
The fish, the frog, the water-snake
The duck, the dolphin and the otter."

"And all us too," interrupted voices from the ceiling, the nooks and the walls.

"Yes, of course...I've just named a few," Agarmagar continued impatiently, "Now, listen carefully: the human beings can save the river if they want to. All they have to do is take some extra trouble and clean the dirty waste water that flows from factories into rivers."

"Dirty waste water? You mean effluents?" asked Jai, now convinced that Agarmagar was a chap who hated homework.

Agarmagar looked surprised. "Yes. They have to clean these effluents," he announced loftily, "By using water treatment plants," hoping to impress the gathering.

"Plants?" asked Diya.

"Oh, that's what they called these machines which can clean huge amounts of water," Jai reminded her.

"Water treatment plants! You have to make each of these factory people use water treatment plants in their factories. You must convince them!"

"Or force them and force them till they listen," added the snake, who wanted results.

The children were enthusiastic to help. There were mixed promises of "We'll try our best- we'll do what we can- let's start now- let's make a plan."

Thunderous applause went out for Jai, Raj and Diya in the Cave of Creation. The water-creatures broke into a noisy din of hopeful speculation.

Agarmagar was pleased with the night's events. "I'll drop you back now like I promised," he yawned, tired by the exertion. "The migratory water birds will be in touch with you. You'll know the flamingoes by their scarlet hue."

The flamingoes waved from the deep corner.

"Goodbye, then!" said Agarmagar to the countless water creatures.

"Goodbye," said the creatures. The gharial left the cave with the children.

"I hope you work on our strategy. Then we'll avoid a huge tragedy," Agarmagar reminded Jai, Raj and Diya as they returned to the raft, the lady and Antaratma, the river-guide.

The children hopped on to the raft, and bade Agarmagar farewell.

"Ha ha! Wasn't that clever!" Agarmagar mused, as he swam away into the moonlit water.

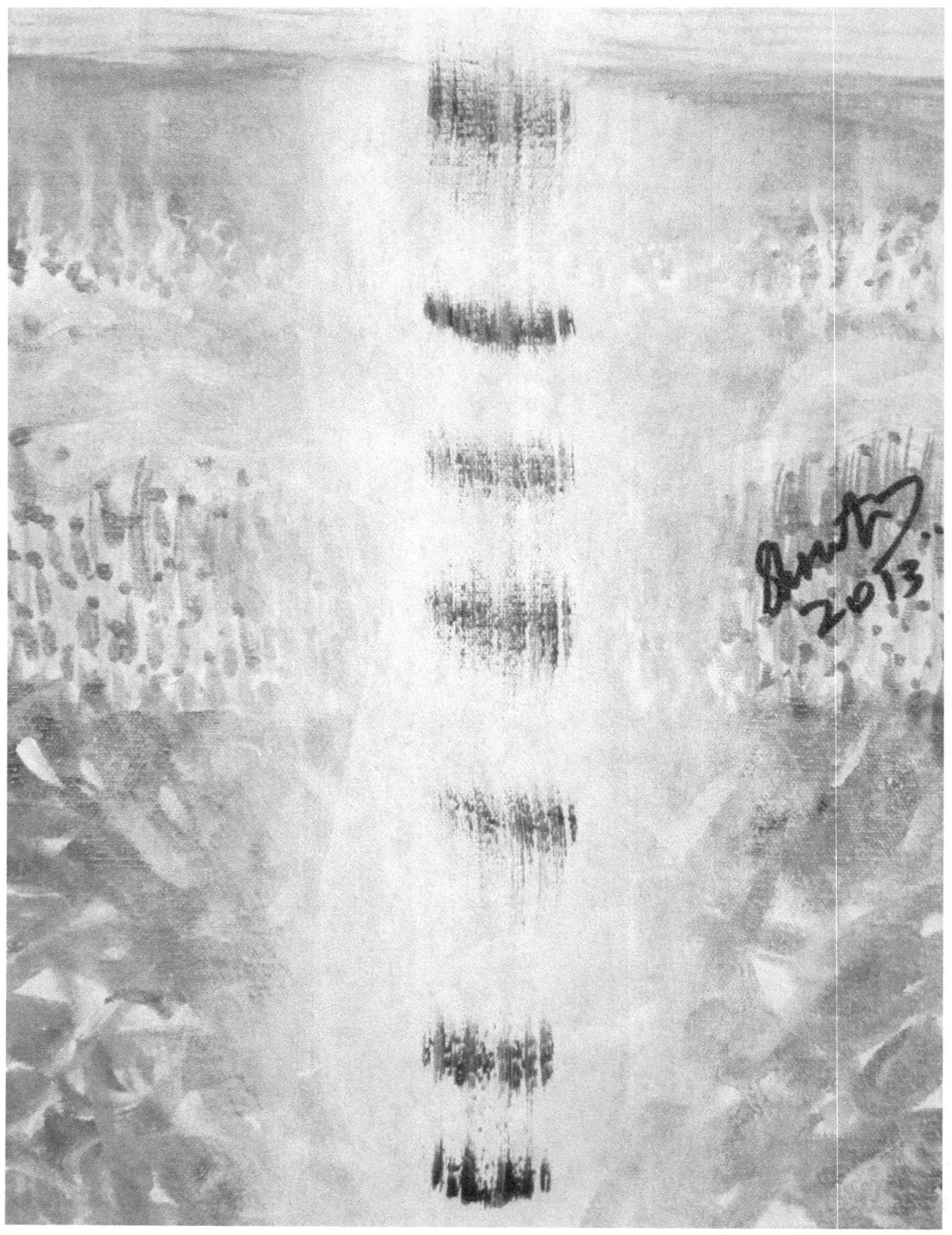

LICKETY-SPLIT!

The Cave of Creation had been left to grapple with the Shadows of Sham. Dawn broke on the rest of the Bahtareen. The Halchalhawa skimmed its surface, spreading mind-altering scents of wild flowers and grasses from the jungle of Hurryburry.

Raj described their recent adventure to the Lady Who Did Not Like Air Conditioners and to Antaratma, the river-guide.

"Hey kids, that must have been quite an adventure!" exclaimed Antar. To their relief, he sounded enthusiastic, and not in the least bit annoyed.

"It was, and we've promised to help the water creatures," said Raj.

"That's great," said Antar. Then his face clouded for a moment as though the Shadows of Sham had suddenly passed by.

"I don't want to frighten you," he said, "But we could be in great danger right now." His words sounded strange on a pleasant, fragrant morning.

"How?" asked Raj.

"Now?" questioned Jai.

"Agarmagar promised not to eat us," offered Diya.

"Oh, it's not about Agarmagar," said Antar.

"We spoke to someone else while you children were away," the lady informed them.

"Who?" asked the children in a chorus.

Before the grown-ups could reply, the children heard a melodious voice singing,

"Lickety-split, my lovelies!"

Which meant hurry up and go away. But it was a kind, mysterious voice, which seemed to possess many hidden qualities.

"Now who was THAT?!" asked Diya loudly, looking all around and not seeing anyone.

"Hey, I can't see anyone around," said Jai.

"Unlikely, unlikely," said the playful voice.

"Who's talking to us?" Diya asked no one in particular. As the waves of the Bahtareen grew stronger, the voice continued,

"You'd like to linger languidly,
You'd love to laze and lounge.
But it looks like-
You'll have to leave like lightning.
Launch away sooner
And there'll be no lacuna."

It was a lilting, melodious sound, but the message was urgent. The voice was asking them to hurry up and go away. It was almost like a warning.

The raft was now running through rough water.

"Launch away sooner, and there'll be no lacuna," repeated the voice.

"You're the river, aren't you?" guessed Diya, who had been listening intently.

"A logical link, my limpkin.
Linger no longer.
Lithological logistics seem to say
I'll have to launch to lofty levels today."

"It means there's going to be a flood," explained the lady.

"A FLOOD?!" exclaimed the children, feeling a little helpless.

"They've built a large dam on the river down-stream," said Antar, looking very serious.

The Bahtareen will overflow from its path and flood the Hurryburry jungle."

"Lucid logic, and I can't do a thing about it," complained the river.

"Those forest people we met will drown," Diya was alarmed.

"They might escape..." said Raj.

"But they'll still lose their homes," the lady said.

"And the temperature of the water will change," added Antar, "All the aquatic creatures will suffer."

"Oh! The water creatures!" Jai's mind raced to the Cave of Creation and the countless creatures. "I wonder if the water creatures' association knows about this. We promised to help the water creatures."

The jungle of Hurryburry usually waits for the rain. But this time, the clouds of rain had brought new shadows of the morning.

Upstream, there were wild claps of thunder. The Halchalhawa raced around, not knowing what to do. It would rain. The new dam would hinder the path of the rainy river. The Bahtareen would flood over, submerging the jungle and the life within.

"We must escape before we're caught in the flood," Antar said, wondering whether the others realized the kind of danger in which they were. "There'll be huge waves," he shouted as the rain-water from upstream rushed down.

"But we have our paddles and our raft," said Diya gleefully, quite certain that nothing would happen to them.

"The tide will be too strong for the raft," Antar replied.

"Lickety-split! I wish I could do something!" fumed a turbulent and unusually infuriated Bahtareen.

"What should we do?" the children could barely be heard above the waves. There were panic-stricken shouts of "What should we do?- oh no!- the water is already getting choppy- help!- what do we do?!"

"We're nearing the dam," boomed Antaratma. It was a miracle that they hadn't fallen off the raft already. This time, it would have been dangerous.

Luckily, they hadn't run out of miracles.

"I'll splash your raft up in one leviathan leap if I can," offered the river. "If you're lucky, you'll land right on top of the lousy dam."

"It's the only chance that we have," agreed Antar. "We'll have to take the chance," shouted the lady.

"Will we make it to the height?
The water's getting rougher,
the green is turning white.
We'll splash-laaand

On the daaam
If we caaan!"

The Bahtareen summoned its deepest reserves of strength. The countless water-creatures gathered to roll the wave that would catapult their messengers of hope. It stretched far into the sky and then receded.

"We're on the dam, ahoy!" called Antar. Stars swam in the air around them from the impact.

"Ow! Our raft landed with quite a thud!" squealed Diya, who liked roller coasters.

"Yes. We can now cross the river," said Antar, "But we'll have to change our plans."

"It's going to be a long walk downhill," said the lady.

"And we'll be walking through dense forests," added Antar.

"What about the flood at the foot of the hill?" asked Jai.

"I know a part that won't get flooded," Antar assured them.

"Get ready for a long walk through the jungle!" the lady said.

It was afternoon. They began their descent of the slope of one of the hills of the Hurryburry jungle.

WE MEET THE THICKET AND GANG

A weak afternoon light dodged the shadows. The Halchalhawa managed to free itself from the shadows of the morning. It hunted for the group in a sudden gale, raking up dried leaves and snapping twigs.

The downward slope of the Hurryburry grabbed the straws of the Halchalhawa.

The Halchalhawa was in search of Jai, Raj, Diya and the grown-ups. Through bushes and thorns it tore, through stumps and abandoned nests, carrying with it, the crusaders of the Hurryburry whose numbers were multiplying.

Dusk was beginning to fall. The Shadows of Sham were beginning to fall again, starker and stronger than before. The Halchalhawa and its crusaders accelerated their search.

The group of human beings trod carefully through Antar's chosen track.

"That tree looks like it's full of stars," said Diya suddenly.

"Where?" Raj wanted to know. "Where?" asked Jai, and then saw the tree.

"Oh! There! I know what those are. They're fireflies."

"Fireflies?" Diya hadn't heard of fireflies.

"Insects that fly about in daaark forrrests," Jai whispered hoarsely, and laughed. Raj chuckled.

"You can't scare me!" said Diya.

"Ouch! Who stepped on my toes?" asked the lady suddenly.

"Not me," each of them replied.

At that instant, the Halchalhawa swirled its way towards the group. The strong wind surrounded them and lifted them off their feet. As they stood mid-air, being blown about amongst the trees, everything seemed awake and agog in this patch of the Hurryburry.

"What's going on?" the lady shouted from mid-air.

"I saw that tree move!" yelled Diya incredulously. "I saw it walk!" she shouted, pointing at one of the many trees that were walking into the clearing, drawn by the Halchalhawa.

"Ha ha! A walking tree!" laughed Jai and Raj, who were sure that the whole thing was a dream. Then they landed on the ground, and found that the trees were still milling around.

"Eek! What's happening? It's a creeper!" screamed Diya.

"Look! She's caught in a creeper!" called Jai in alarm.

"What on earth is going on?" Antar addressed the trees.

"I think we've walked into some thick bushes. Couldn't see them," said the lady.

"No. LOOK!" said Antar, "There are plants walking towards us." "We've been surrounded by them!" gasped Jai.

The trees looked menacing. The lady recognized a few mango trees who were also known as the Aamjunta and a peepul tree that occasionally allowed writers to meet it. There were many others who were surging forward.

"We are the trees who ran away from the flood, and we're very angry with all you human beings. You're destroying us and our forests. Don't you realize that you need plants around you for your own good?" they growled contemptuously.

"Of course we do," replied the lady, "We're on your side."

"Oh, we don't believe you," the trees retorted.

It wasn't funny at all. The creepers imprisoned the children, the lady and Antar. They formed complicated knots, and the human beings stood there, bound and unable to move.

"We're usually a peace-loving thicket
But we've been put on a really sticky wicket,"
rasped the thicket of trees.

The Halchalhawa hadn't expected this extreme action. It tried reasoning with the trees that were now in constant movement.

"We don't wanna fight, you know
But we can't take this anymore,"

they explained to the Halchalhawa. Then, they marched around the group triumphantly, singing,
"You burn us trees,
Do as you please,
You cause a flood,
Erode the mud.
-Have you gone crazy?"

The lady was very annoyed. So were the children and Antar.

The creepers that had trussed them were pokey, itchy, and cut into their skin. Antar disapproved of the violent actions of the trees.

All of a sudden, the trees on the slope of the Hurryburry bowed low.

"Ah! The rest of the gang's here."

The outlawed king of the forest strode in, accompanied by his compatriots. He had spotted his followers and their prisoners.

"It's the disgruntled tiger with the boar, the birds and the deer," Antar whispered to the lady. She had heard of the powers of the outlawed king of the Hurryburry. He had started by fighting for a just cause. The Hurryburry and the forest people had rallied behind him and offered his comrades shelter.

But things were now going beyond the control of reason.

"Gang, we've found a bunch of humans!" laughed the mighty one. The night grew darker as the Shadows of Sham gathered to genuflect at his paws.

"We've found a bunch of humans!!!" he roared again, amused by the terror that appeared on their faces.

"We're telling them what we think of them," the thicket of trees informed him. Then, they barked and snapped at the humans,

"We don't wanna fight, you know.
But we can't take this anymore.
You shoot these guys.
You think you're wise.
Disturbing us.
We'll make a fuss.
-Of course, we will."

"But all human beings are not cruel. We want to help you," said the lady, trying not to lose her patience. There they stood, on one of the slopes of the extreme wings of the Hurryburry.

The Striped One and his comrades were aware that time was short in the jungle of Hurryburry. The forest people had been complaining about the accelerated destruction of the elements. The Halchalhawa had conveyed this to the striped one.

The mighty Striped One knew that it would be difficult to hold out without the support of the forest people. The ruthless city was in hot pursuit of the Striped One and his comrades. This was a scent that he had picked up from the Halchalhawa.

The Striped One toyed with the idea of effecting a compromise. He knew that Jai, Raj, Diya and even the two grown-ups were genuinely interested in saving the planet of the Hurryburry.

Indeed, reports of the water creatures' meeting had reached him many hours ago. His secret agents, the underground springs of the Bahtareen, had strongly recommended peaceful means for the future. The underground streams were of the distilled view that in the days to come, the children would be able to improve the condition of the Hurryburry. They were the jungle's link to the world outside, the secret agents asserted.

A flamingo had been hiding behind his comrades. He wasn't sure of how he'd be treated if the Striped One found out that he knew the children. But it was now apparent that the Striped One was aware of nearly all of the happenings within the Hurryburry, at least.

"Hey, I recognize these kids!" volunteered the flamingo. The widely-traveled bird felt that this was the ideal opportunity for the striped one to relax his stance.

"Oh! Flamingo of the scarlet hue, weren't you at the water creatures' meeting too?" asked Jai, relieved to see that matters might be resolved, after all.

"Yes, indeed," confirmed the flamingo.

The Striped One nodded.

"They're on our side, folks!" announced the flamingo who had traveled far and wide and wore scarlet and pink feathers.

"Oh, well, if you say so," mumbled the thicket of trees. They were not too pleased about having to free their captives.

The Halchalhawa sighed a sigh of relief.

Before the thicket and his followers could react, the Striped One turned to the children.

"Alright, so what's the plan?" the Striped One demanded to know.

A plan had been brewing in their minds since the water creatures' meeting.

"We think you should invade the city," said Jai, Raj and Diya.

"You mean, start a war with the human beings?" asked the Striped One, surprised.

"Oh no, not a war!" Raj said with certainty.

"Nothing dangerous or harmful," said Diya.

"You homeless trees should go and stick your roots into the ground in the city," explained Jai.

"And then the rest of us could follow," said the Striped One, approvingly.

"And not harm the human beings, of course," Antar sought a clarification.

"No harm will be done," the Striped One assured them.

"It's a wonderful idea," the lady was very enthusiastic.

But Antar still had reservations.

"You know, the city people might try to chase you away. They might harm you. It's a dangerous plan. And you might not like the city."

"We're not going there to like the city, we're going there to change it!" roared the Striped One.

The sun flared into the sky. A soft drizzle and a rainbow floated on its magical rays.

"One needs to fight for things that matter.
Good stuff doesn't come on a silver platter," sang the gang,
"We'll brave the city."

"And what if our plan doesn't work?" asked the peepul tree.

"Well, that'll be a pity."

The Striped One looked at Antar through the corner of his eye.

"But we'll know we've tried. Don't you agree, river-guide?" "Actually, I do," answered Antar.

"Let's waste no time," they all shouted,
"Let's start our march
From this hill to the city's arch.

Let's romp and rustle into the city's hustle.
Lets make our way to the city's bustle."

Jai, Raj, Diya, the lady, Antar and the trees walked through the arched rainbow and eventually reached the golden arches of the city's gates.

THE CITY OF HAZAARBAZAAR

The trees and the children were good friends by the time they reached the city of Hazaarbazaar. The aamjunta trees from the jungle of Hurryburry were dazed by the kaliedescopic lights of the city.

Maroon and purple and gold and orange lights darted into the darkness. They felt giddy and were already half-choked by the factory fumes that had assailed them on the outskirts.

There weren't too many people on the roads at that hour. Some did notice the strange walking trees, but the thicket evaded them with the help of the children, the lady and Antar.

News now travels in the city nearly as swiftly as it does on the Bahtareen. It is transmitted to outer space, and from there, is distributed to the citizens of Hazaarbazaar.

The lights of the city of Hazaarbazaar went out. The city rotated away from the banished moon.

The citizens awoke. Many performed the curious task of making their way towards their television sets and switching them on with their eyes closed. They did this with a sense of yogic achievement.

Then, they sat up when they heard the first snatches of the unusual telecast.
"The news, brought to you by Citysmart. A group of trees that have escaped the floods seem to have stormed into the capital city. We spoke to a few people who saw this happen."

A garble of interviews followed in mixed tongues, with subtitles whose meaning appeared too bizarre to be even an approximation of the original.
Then the solemn voice continued, "These people claim that three children were seen running through the city with a group of trees. Some tried chasing them. A villager who now lives in the city says that she has not seen such a sight even in her own village. We managed to secretly record the latest activities of this unusual group. Here is what we have...." said the earnest-solemn voice, now sounding triumphant.

From behind bushes, the camera zoomed in on the children, the lady and Antar. They were seen against a backdrop of abundant foliage. Neon hoardings illuminated the market circle.

"The city is asleep," whispered Raj, "This is the market circle."
"Strange", thought the cameraman, as Raj seemed to address the hidden camera.
"You can look into the shop windows, trees!" Diya said.
A surprised cameraman fell backwards as his curtain of bushes rushed

towards the shop windows.
"What's this?" the peepul tree asked.

The children realized that they were being shot on camera. Their minds worked quickly, and in unison. They all pretended not to have noticed the rolling cameraman.

"It's a furniture shop," Jai announced, his voice ringing loud and clear.
"Furniture? -huh- made of wood from trees, of course!" wheezed the tired thicket of trees, winking secretly at the children.
"And what's that?" they asked.
"Oh, that's a book shop," volunteered Raj.
"Books made of paper from trees? We've heard about this stuff," rasped the trees.
"Don't be angry. We NEED furniture and we NEED books," reasoned Jai.
"Oh, we don't mind that," said the trees, also playing to the imaginary audience. They arranged themselves in geometrical formations and gyrated about in synchronized movements.

It was different from the dance of the forest people, and unlike anything that had ever been witnessed in the jungle of Hurryburry.
They were out to conquer. They sang,
"You can chop some trees for wood.
In fact, I think you should.
You can chop some trees for paper.
I'm not a paper-book hater.
But why should you be greedy?
I don't think they'll be needy
If they recycle stuff....
Isn't one chair enough?
- How many chairs are they going to sit on?"

"I don't need a chair," grinned Diya.
"I'm feeling thirsty," the peepul tree interrupted, "I need to plant my

roots into the ground for water."
"There's no mud for plants to grow.
No space for water to flow
into the ground.
There's cement all around," Antar said, sounding grim.

The trees were dehydrated. They began to droop. Then the Halchalhawa zoomed in, carrying reserves of moisture. The brief spell of pleasant weather enthused them. Once again, they danced for the hidden, unsuspecting camera, singing:

"Let's break this concrete.
Let's plant ourselves.
Let's be this city's evergreen elves.
And every noon,
When the grown-ups sleep,
Into those playrooms and nurseries we'll creep.
The city's kids will listen to our tales
Of jungles and rivers and of distant vales.
And very soon, there'll be a day
When the city will invite the jungle to stay."

"Do you mean we're going to turn the city into a jungle?" Diya inquired. "Not exactly," replied the trees. "There'll still be schools and hospitals and shops, but they'll all look very different."

Antar and the lady looked relieved. They did not want to create panic in the city of Hazaarbazaar with its gluttonous consumers.

"Now, back to the news," enunciated the earnest person, "Everyone waits anxiously while these three kids, this group of trees, and it is rumoured, their other secret friends from the forest, work on changing the city and the world.

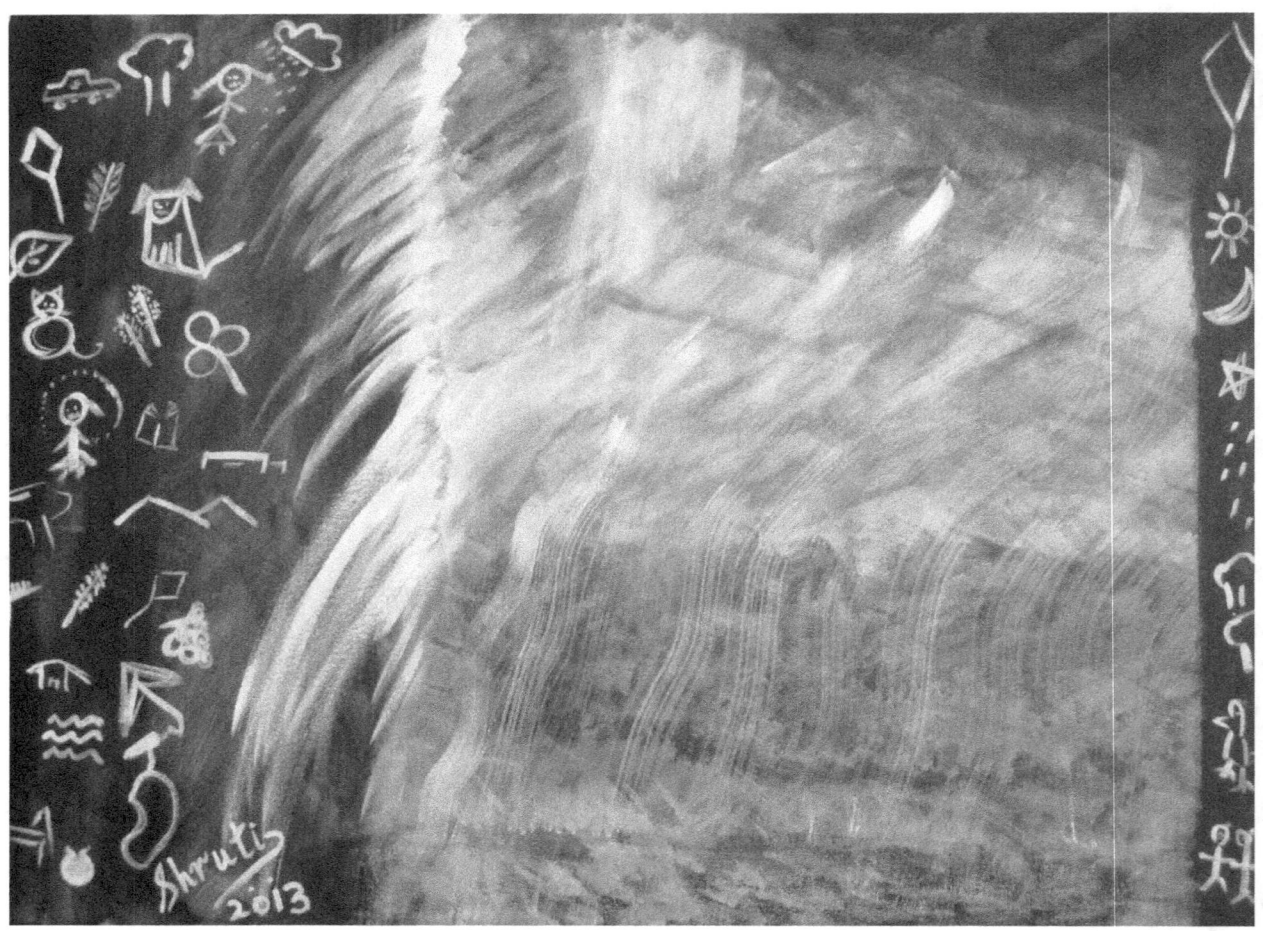

THERE'LL BE A RADICAL CHANGE

Strange winds are known to tear through the streets of Hazaarbazaar. In the summer, eddies of dust from afar skim across rippling mirages. The blazing outdoor turns fearsome. People retire towards the reassuring scents of regulated temperature and drawn blinds.

Those who are without are seen teeming with grit and resilience. Sometimes, they run on clockwork. Many lie scattered and wilting. In the winter, equal and opposite winds bite into those same hides.

The city of Hazaarbazaar pulsates with coloured light. Gleaming metal and hard faces stalk its roads. Fat wallets and plastic cards are held out as shields and weapons, as wands of wizardry to the world. The elements are fought with this armour, fraught by a lurking fear and a need for insulation. Ruthless means justify terror-driven ends. Thereafter, the annihilation of the other is easily brought about to add to the feathery trinkets that must couch the human form.

The children and the forces of the Hurryburry plunged into this gluttonous tunnel of the Hazaarbazaar. They struggled from moonrise to moonset and from sunrise again.

Their days did not end. They wove stories of the jungle. Of the symbiosis of beings, of the elements. They spoke and they argued. They demonstrated and they pleaded. The Halchalhawa swung into action.

People shivered with the hope from the jungle. Their minds gathered strength from hours of wandering through the green shade of the trees of the Hurryburry. Those who could hear the echoes of the Striped One were not frightened, but felt inspired.

The euphoria caused great alarm amongst the Ruthless ones of the Hazaarbazaar. They directed one of their minions, a robot named Ahem, to pilfer information, and to demotivate the children.

"What have the trees been telling you?" it asked the citizens.

"They talk about forests,
they talk about fires,
they talk about smoke, and they…"

"It's all a big joke, they're nasty little liars," rasped Ahem.
This defied logic. "Who? The trees?" asked the citizens, "We don't think so."
"They tell you that you can change the world. My calculations say that that's not possible."

"But it is!" insisted the citizens, "We can do little things AND we can do big things."
"Little things like what?" asked Ahem.

"We can recycle things like papers and cans. We can save electricity by switching off extra fans," they replied.
"Could we leave ACs on instead?" asked Diya.

Just then, the trees and the gang from the Hurryburry walked in, singing,

"Air conditioners are bad for the atmosphere.
They blow a hole in the ozone layer.
Did the stone age man use an air conditioning fan?
Does the thirstiest ostrich drink water from a fridge?
Does the jungle cat wear a designer hat?
Do the swans at dusk use perfumes of musk?
Does the silliest fox keep a jewel box?
Then why do you???!!!!"

Jai addressed Ahem,
"We are going to change people's minds! We're going to make them treat the earth and everything on it differently."

"What are you going to do and say?" Ahem questioned.

"Recycle, don't waste, don't be greedy, plant trees, don't pollute. We'll spread the word!"

"Won't the world move backwards instead of forward?" prodded Ahem the robot.

"Not at all!" the children sang.
"Not at all
The world won't stall.
There'll be a radical change."

And they knew they couldn't be wrong.

Already, the law-makers of the city were thinking. They had woken up one morning to see lush greenery outside their windows. Then they noticed that the words on everyone's lips in the fatigued city of Hazaarbazaar were,

"There'll be a radical change.
The world will look strange to you.
This is how it'll be.
This is how it'll be.
You'll see.
They'll say
Long, long ago, there was a time
Maybe it was nineteen ninetynine,
When things got bad.
Really, really bad.
Then, the children changed everything they could.
Now things are good.
Really, really good.
Long, long ago, there was a time.
Maybe it was nineteen ninety nine...."

The logical robot plodded its heavy way back to the den of the Ruthless Ones. "Ahem…" it reported, "There'll be a radical change...."

-Written in the year 1999 by V. Shruti Devi

The art-works and photography in this publication are by V. Shruti Devi.

Titles of art-works:

Chalice

Prajjallara

The People of the Eastern Ghaats

Intangibles

Aum Chanting

Ground Water (clay modeling and mixed media installation art)

Quite Something

Asukha Po

Sufi Mor

This version of Creatures of the Current by V. Shruti Devi published with Create Space, 2015.

V. Shruti Devi, born in Madras, India, on the 30th of December, 1972, is a political leader, lawyer, social activist, free-lance writer, poet and Princess of Kurupam.